Week 1

Active Listening

People naturally contact customer service with a "crisis" or "concern", looking for guidance, information, and most importantly...comfort. It's very important to understand that for some customers, just lending them your ear is customer service in itself. Incorporate active listening into your daily customer service routine (listen more than talk) and you will be surprised how much of a difference this small gesture makes on the rapport with your customers.

"Listening is an art that requires attention over talent, spirit over ego, others over self."

Week 1

Applied Knowledge

_____
_____
_____
_____
_____
_____
_____
_____
_____
_____

Results

_____
_____
_____
_____
_____
_____
_____
_____
_____
_____

Week 2

Probing Questions

To identify to the "T" what each customer is inquiring about, the most effective method to use is to ask probing questions. The best questions to ask are "clarification" questions (ie. "so, what you are asking is....", "to make sure I have this correct, you are calling to..., etc.).

There are numerous times where customers go on rants or tangents that can confuse you along the way as to what the purpose of their inquiry truly is. The tactic of asking questions not only allows you to diagnose the situation to provide the correct answer, but also affirms to the customer that you are attentive and engaged in their concerns.

"Asking questions doesn't mean you don't know your job, asking questions means you want to improve the quality of your work."

Week 2

Applied Knowledge

_____
_____
_____
_____
_____
_____
_____
_____
_____
_____

Results

_____
_____
_____
_____
_____
_____
_____
_____
_____

Week 3

The Power of Positive Perspective

The essential nature of customer service is to aid and advise those who purchase or use our products or services. One of the most useful tactics to help achieve high quality customer service is to answer each call with a positive outcome in mind. We want to find ways to say "yes" before an ultimate answer of "no" is given.

Remember, our thoughts, feelings, and emotions reflect in our voices and actions, and because of this, the demeanor we project greatly affects our environment. Having a positive perspective when you handle customer concerns initiates a higher probability of positive responses, which in turn can greatly affect the outcome of your interaction.

"Once you replace negative thoughts with positive ones, you'll start having positive results."

Week 3

Applied Knowledge

_____
_____
_____
_____
_____
_____
_____
_____
_____
_____

Results

_____
_____
_____
_____
_____
_____
_____
_____
_____
_____

Week 4

Be Interested

Some customer service jobs can be very monotonous, such as telephone customer service. So, to keep it fresh and new on each interaction, try taking a genuine interest in each customer's unique situation. If you take a genuine interest in the customer's question or concerns, you will make the process more enjoyable for both you and the customer.

At times, customer service can be taxing mentally and emotionally, so we want to try anything we can to be able to keep our minds in order. Incorporating an exercise such as this will help you keep your mind healthy and sharp.

"Concentration and mental toughness are the margins of victory"

Week 4

Applied Knowledge

_____
_____
_____
_____
_____
_____
_____
_____
_____
_____

Results

_____
_____
_____
_____
_____
_____
_____
_____
_____
_____

Week 5

The C.A.R.P. Method

When dealing with sensitive situations, we must give credence to our customers' complaints, though not all complaints indicate an issue. A great way to help stay consistent in tone and process is by using the C.A.R.P. method:

- **Control** the situation
- **Acknowledge** the dilemma
- **Refocus** the conversation
- **Problem-solve** so the customer leaves happy

Using this method, you will be able to convey concern, attentiveness, and a genuine sense of care with your customer, as well as overcome the "tough" parts in a conversation so that it ends on a good note, leading to better rapport.

"True empathy is the ability to step into the shoes of another person, aiming to understand their feelings, and perspectives, and to use that understanding to guide our actions"

Week 5

Applied Knowledge

_____
_____
_____
_____
_____
_____
_____
_____
_____
_____

Results

_____
_____
_____
_____
_____
_____
_____
_____
_____
_____

Week 6

The 5 C's

Good communication and customer service can vary based on the uniqueness of each situation, however there are always 5 basic components to good communication. It should be:

- **Clear**
- **Complete**
- **Concise**
- **Concrete**
- **Correct**

You should always make sure that with any customer communication the client understands your explanation or solution by stating it clearly, describing it briefly but completely, in terms that are specific and, importantly, that you have all of your facts correct to ensure you always leave a good impression.

"The quality of your communication is the quality of your life."

Week 6

Applied Knowledge

_____
_____
_____
_____
_____
_____
_____
_____
_____
_____

Results

_____
_____
_____
_____
_____
_____
_____
_____
_____
_____
_____

Week 7

<u>Giving Spoken Feedback Signals</u>

All customer service, whether face-to-face or via any other kind of media it is highly important that the client is kept aware that you are still "engaged" or paying attention, by using spoken feedback signals.

These are just a combination of different words and short phrases to acknowledge that you heard and understand what the caller has said. Most commonly used is the "mirroring back" method where you acknowledge the client by repeating what they just said while following along with the conversation. This method will not only show the customer that you are attentive, but it will also open the door for you to show empathy, concern or interest in what the caller is saying.

"The quality of your communication is the quality of your life."

Week 7

Applied Knowledge

Results

Week 8

Under Promise, Over Deliver

For one to maintain a higher quality of customer service, one must set clear expectations for our customers. What you **NEVER** want to do is make promises you can't keep. Using the tactic of under promising and over delivering is a great tool to help promote our company's efficiency as well as leave our customers with a positive experience.

You should only ever offer a customer or client something that you are sure you can give them, and when you do offer it to them, leave them with an expectation that it will take longer than it actually will to get it done. You will always **WIN** in this scenario, while looking like a hero at the same time to the customer when you over deliver on your promises.

"When you make a commitment, you build hope. When you keep it, you build trust."

Week 8

Applied Knowledge

_____
_____
_____
_____
_____
_____
_____
_____
_____
_____

Results

_____
_____
_____
_____
_____
_____
_____
_____
_____
_____

Week 9

Be Memorably Good

If you do not create an experience for your customers that is memorable, your story will not spread. If you think about it, customer service is essentially as much a marketing tool as advertisement is. It can make and break a company depending on its quality. So, with that in mind, make every customer interaction an experience to remember in a positive way so that your story can be heard by others who may be looking for a service like yours.

"One day you'll just be a memory to some people. Do your best to be a good one."

Week 9

Applied Knowledge

_____
_____
_____
_____
_____
_____
_____
_____
_____

Results

_____
_____
_____
_____
_____
_____
_____
_____
_____

Week 10

Know Your Audience

As customer service representatives, we encounter a wide array of individuals who have their own unique personalities, experiences and up-bringings. This implies that there is no "ONE TYPE" of customer we deal with. With that in mind, we should never approach them with "ONE TYPE" of service. Use the following skills to assist you with discerning who you are interacting with so you can better "gel" with your callers to improve in service:

1. **LISTEN**- Your best assets are your ears. You have the ability to allow your callers to reveal what type of person you are dealing with, early, just by listening to how they speak.

2. **IDENTIFY COMMONALITIES**- Relating to people leads to comfort. If you can see where your caller is coming from, you have a higher possibility of connecting with that individual.

3. **BE FAMILIAR**- Being approachable softens any blows. Try to deliver information in a "down to earth" manner, rather than in robotic, "scripted" sounded responses. This will help to bridge the humanistic connection between you and the customer.

"Connection is the energy that is created between people when they feel seen, heard, and valued."

Week 10

Applied Knowledge

_____
_____
_____
_____
_____
_____
_____
_____
_____
_____

Results

_____
_____
_____
_____
_____
_____
_____
_____
_____
_____

Week 11

Time is Relative

One of the most revolutionary concepts that we learned in the 20th century is that time is not a universal measurement. The rate at which it passes depends entirely on your speed and acceleration at any given moment. Keeping this in mind, utilizing proper time management (ie. short holds, explaining to the customer what you are doing, setting time frame expectations, etc.) while delivering your customer service will create an effective way to gather all information needed, and help make the process flow smoothly. Find that rhythm and keep doing it, consistently.

"If you want to be more productive, you need to become master of your minutes."

Week 11

Applied Knowledge

_____
_____
_____
_____
_____
_____
_____
_____
_____
_____

Results

_____
_____
_____
_____
_____
_____
_____
_____
_____
_____

Week 12

Never Take the Bait

Though we would like to believe that all interactions we have with our customers will be amazing, easy, and comforting, this notion is not always the case in the realm of customer service. There will be times where the customer uses derogatory phrases intended to spark confrontation.

DO NOT TAKE THE BAIT!!

These are tactics used by the customer intended to direct the conversation's course towards a verbal quarrel. When you "take the bait", to that individual, they have won, and you have lost. You can divert these actions by cordially continuing the conversation as originally started, without feeding into the comments.

"It is not the strongest of the species that survives, nor the most intelligent that survives. It is the one that is the most adaptable to change."

Week 12

Applied Knowledge

Results

Week 13

Facilitation Determination

Sounds like an old after school educational special (conjunction junction...lol), however, this is actually an important tool in customer service. Discerning the correct place to facilitate the concerns of the client plays a critical role in excellent customer service. You never want to provide callers with a "next step" that does not directly address their specific concerns.

By correctly facilitating the customer's concerns, you avoid adding an additional unnecessary step that can potentially create more issues in the long run.

"Efficiency is doing better what is already being done."

Week 13

Applied Knowledge

_____
_____
_____
_____
_____
_____
_____
_____
_____
_____
_____

Results

_____
_____
_____
_____
_____
_____
_____
_____
_____
_____

Week 14

Avoiding Negativity

While engaged in a conversation with a caller, you should always be cognizant of your responses, more so of any NEGATIVE responses. You should practice conscientious avoidance of:

1. Raising your voice
2. Sarcasm
3. Indifference
4. Rudely interrupting the caller
5. Making any statement indicating that you "can not" or "will not" help

Always think before you speak, and steer far away from any confrontational phrases such as comments that place blame on the caller or lead to verbal finger pointing. This will increase your ability to build a respectful rapport with the caller, leading to a satisfying phone conversation.

"Candor is a proof of both a just frame of mind, and of a good tone of breeding. It is a quality that belongs equally to the honest man and to the gentleman."

Week 14

Applied Knowledge

_____
_____
_____
_____
_____
_____
_____
_____
_____

Results

_____
_____
_____
_____
_____
_____
_____
_____
_____

Week 15

Client Appreciation

Part of our job as customer service representatives includes demonstrating appreciation for our clients' time and business. This can be achieved, not only by thanking them directly, but also by exceeding their expectations and going above and beyond to satisfy them. Creating successful outcomes for our clients can be thought of as an opportunity to improve the process, providing end-of-line resolutions.

Remember, our clients (whether customers, agents, etc.) are the reason we are here. Show them we appreciate them by making each call your BEST!!

"Appreciation can make a day, even change a life. Your willingness to put it into words is all that is necessary."

Week 15

Applied Knowledge

_____
_____
_____
_____
_____
_____
_____
_____
_____
_____

Results

_____
_____
_____
_____
_____
_____
_____
_____
_____
_____

Week 16

Providing Alternatives

When dealing with customers, naturally, you may run into some obstacles along the way. As customer service representatives, we should be cognizant that not all solutions offered will be understood or accepted. Providing additional alternatives to the customer to help reach the desired solution may give you the opportunity to overcome some of these obstacles, if feasible. As in human nature, when provided with choices, we are more compelled to choose one of those choices, rather than being presented with one solution, where the choice is to take it or leave it.

"Challenges are what make life interesting. Overcoming them is what makes them meaningful."

Week 16

Applied Knowledge

_____
_____
_____
_____
_____
_____
_____
_____
_____
_____
_____
_____

Results

_____
_____
_____
_____
_____
_____
_____
_____
_____
_____
_____
_____

Week 17

Ask vs. Demand

"Give me your...", "you need to provide me with...". These phrases can easily be received as being too forward, and quite frankly harsh. "May I have your...", "To resolve your issue, I would ask that you provide me with...". These phrases are less curt or abrupt, therefore are much more palatable to the ear, while giving the customer a sense of a choice in the matter.

When you are the PROVIDER of information/solutions, the way you convey customer compliance requirements is crucial for generating a positive interaction/outcome. Resolution without courtesy is no resolution at all.

"You will accomplish more by kind words and a courteous manner than by anger or sharp rebuke, which should never be used except in necessity."

Week 17

Applied Knowledge

_____
_____
_____
_____
_____
_____
_____
_____
_____
_____

Results

_____
_____
_____
_____
_____
_____
_____
_____
_____
_____

Week 18

Written Tone

Excellent customer service not only should be considered when dealing with clients face to face or over the phone, but also in our written correspondences. Because it is difficult to determine tone over email, text, chat or any other form of written information, understand that our choice of words, and the tone they carry, are crucial when it comes to our readers' interpretation.

Try using a polite and informative tone in your text, "killing them with kindness", so to speak. This will not only help to convey strong competency in the matter but will also help reduce tension with frustrated clients you may come across.

"When you change the way you look at things, the things you look at change."

Week 18

Applied Knowledge

_____
_____
_____
_____
_____
_____
_____
_____
_____
_____

Results

_____
_____
_____
_____
_____
_____
_____
_____
_____
_____

Week 19

Timeliness is Key

Not all customer service matters can be handled in one instance. There will be times where review of documentation/customer history, or resolution determinations require us to place clients on hold or schedule a follow up. If this is the case, returning to the customer must be timely. You do not want the customer to wait longer than necessary, or advised, to receive a response. Understand what your client's expectation is with regards to this return information and deliver as expected.

"The greatest gift you can give someone is your time, because when you give your time, you are giving a portion of your life that you will never get back."

Week 19

Applied Knowledge

_____
_____
_____
_____
_____
_____
_____
_____
_____
_____

Results

_____
_____
_____
_____
_____
_____
_____
_____
_____

Week 20

Stick to Plain English

When information given to customers is not clearly understood, what we say to others may allow for open interpretation, which can draw you further away from the customer and their concern(s). To better communicate to customers, we want to avoid any technical terms, jargon or acronyms that the customer may not understand, or know. Being as professionally clear and transparent as possible always leads to better customer service, and communication in general.

Make sure to LEAVE OUT any overly technical terms when communicating with customers.

"Good communication does not mean that you have to speak in perfectly formed sentences and paragraphs. It isn't about slickness. Simple and clear go a long way."

Week 20

Applied Knowledge

_____
_____
_____
_____
_____
_____
_____
_____
_____
_____

Results

_____
_____
_____
_____
_____
_____
_____
_____
_____
_____

Week 21

Keeping it Professional

When handling any customer service situation, a balanced level of professionalism throughout the assistance is required. This can be displayed in many ways, such as deterring from the use of slang in our communication, or addressing the customer as Mr./Mrs./Ms. And their last name. A well-balanced level of professionalism will allow you to be seen as a respectful and knowledgeable companion to the customer, rather than a stranger.

"Professionalism: It's not the job you do, it's how you do the job."

Week 21

Applied Knowledge

_____
_____
_____
_____
_____
_____
_____
_____
_____
_____

Results

_____
_____
_____
_____
_____
_____
_____
_____
_____
_____

Week 22

Stay Neutral

The best customer service representatives never include their personal opinions or biases in conversations with clients. Since we are all different, certain opinions may not bode will with some as they may with others, which can make providing adequate assistance difficult. Keeping a neutral position, while empathizing with the customer will help you arrive at a solution to your customer's concerns in a smooth, courteous and more efficient manner.

"Balance is not better time management but better boundary management."

Week 22

Applied Knowledge

_____
_____
_____
_____
_____
_____
_____
_____
_____
_____
_____

Results

_____
_____
_____
_____
_____
_____
_____
_____
_____
_____
_____

Week 23

1 Step Back, 2 Steps Forward

As individuals, each of us possess our own, personalized way of understanding, thinking, and acting that makes us all unique. This means that not all information you provide in your customer service will be interpreted or perceived in the way you may have intended or would've understood. Therefore, it is always important to re-iterate in more detail what was already advised, to move forward with the call…1 step back, 2 steps forward. It takes a lot of training to understand the nuances of different customers but being able to discern HOW information is being taken and adjusting your delivery to match it is what separates the good from the BEST in customer service.

"People don't ever think from the other person's perspective. If you did you might understand someone more."

Week 23

Applied Knowledge

_____
_____
_____
_____
_____
_____
_____
_____
_____
_____

Results

_____
_____
_____
_____
_____
_____
_____
_____
_____
_____

Week 24

Never Interrupt

The most important part of customer service is listening, which can only be achieved when you do not speak. Allowing the customer to speak without interruption gives assurance that you are taking the customer's call seriously, calms irate customers, gives you a broader picture of the situation, and may ultimately lead the customer to their own answer. This is one of the MOST effective strategies in customer service to help handle ANY inquiry and should be a staple point in your customer service skill set.

"Don't persuade, defend or interrupt. Be curious, be conversational, be real...and listen."

Week 24

Applied Knowledge

_____
_____
_____
_____
_____
_____
_____
_____
_____
_____
_____

Results

_____
_____
_____
_____
_____
_____
_____
_____
_____
_____
_____

Week 25

Admit, Then Fix, Mistakes

There is no such thing as "perfect", especially when it comes to describing people, so it's inevitable that mistakes will be made. If you have made a mistake, you should acknowledge it, apologize then quickly correct it, explaining the steps you have taken to correct the issue. This will provide a better sense of trust and comfortability between you and the customer, especially when you show that you have taken their problem seriously.

"The most honorable people of all are not those who never make mistakes, but those who admit to them when they do, and then go on to do their best to make right the wrongs they made."

Week 25

Applied Knowledge

_____
_____
_____
_____
_____
_____
_____
_____
_____
_____

Results

_____
_____
_____
_____
_____
_____
_____
_____
_____
_____

Week 26

Give Honest Answers

A level of honesty and integrity is required when dealing with customers. After all, the acceptance of the service you provide to your customers will ultimately be based on trust (do I believe this person and the information I've been given?). With this in mind, an expert customer service representative should NEVER lie, guess or make up an answer. Instead, the representative should advise the client that their inquiry is a very good one, and you will check your resources to find the answer or get them to someone who can further assist them. The client will appreciate your honesty and effort to further assist more than you providing an answer that may not help them, or even worse, be completely incorrect.

"Honesty is the fastest way to prevent a mistake from turning into a failure."

Week 26

Applied Knowledge

_____
_____
_____
_____
_____
_____
_____
_____
_____
_____

Results

_____
_____
_____
_____
_____
_____
_____
_____
_____
_____

Week 27

Adding a Personal Touch

Based on my own personal experience and feedback from other customers, not too many people enjoy conversations with what is referred to as a "robot". Instead of delivering information in the manner that Robot B9 would in "Lost in Space" (Danger, Danger Will Robinson!), add your own personal touch to the conversation to build a sense of trust that will assist you with better understanding your clients. Addressing customers by their names, giving verbal recognition queues and simply just being yourself shows clients that you value them as customers and as people.

"Appearances make impressions but it is the personality that makes an impact."

Week 27

Applied Knowledge

Results

Week 28

Be Courteous

Courtesy: The showing of politeness in one's attitude and behavior toward others.
Courtesy is essential to customer service because it leaves a lasting positive impression that may influence one to do business or continue business with you or your company. Smiling while you talk, using respectful and considerate words and phrases, and speaking with excitement are all effective tools that can be used to show courtesy, helping to build a positive, healthy rapport with your clients.

"Courteousness is consideration for others; politeness is the method used to deliver such considerations."

Week 28

Applied Knowledge

Results

Week 29

Know Your Boundaries

Whether it's face-to-face customer service or not, you must always "keep the right distance" when handling your clients. An expert customer service representative will always be aware of their customer's comfort zone, and be able to adjust their behavior, "distance", accordingly. Staying within those boundaries will help you deliver more effective customer service that the client will appreciate.

"Boundaries are not meant to control others they are meant to be used as guidelines for you to know what is acceptable and what is not in your life."

Week 29

Applied Knowledge

Results

Week 30

Reading Cues

Problem-solving skills are required in customer service, and one of the most valuable skills to have is identifying "cues" the client gives when something is unclear and using those cues to get a better idea on how you can help that person. For example, an accountant may require you to go into more detail in explanation, while a truck driver may only be concerned with the answer itself. Understanding the nuances of different clients takes a lot of training, but it will instill strong problem-solving abilities in you that will help mold you into an expert customer service representative.

"It takes a wise man to learn from his mistakes, but an even wiser man to learn from others."

Week 30

Applied Knowledge

_____
_____
_____
_____
_____
_____
_____
_____
_____
_____

Results

_____
_____
_____
_____
_____
_____
_____
_____
_____
_____

Week 31

Using the Right Tools

Now a days, customer service is not just simply smiling and being friendly to clients. With so much that happens in the world of customer service, and the advancement in technology, you should always have and use any "tools" you may have at your disposal to enable you to deliver excellent customer service. Use any reference guides, manuals, guideline sheets, training material or any other resources available to better serve your clients in an effective and efficient manner.

"Even the simplest tools can empower people to do great things."

Week 31

Applied Knowledge

Results

Week 32

Be the Customer

We have all experienced times where we've received sub-par customer service, as well as excellent customer service. Simple situations just not handled correctly, or complex issues that have been taken care of with ease. Whichever side of the spectrum, I'm sure you've seen it all. So, when providing others with customer service, BE the customer. Re-visit your own personal experiences with customer service and use them to guide you where and how YOU would prefer to get information. This not only teaches self-awareness but can greatly improve the outcome of your interactions with clients.

"Always put yourself in the other's shoes. If you feel that it hurts you, it probably hurts the person too."

Week 32

Applied Knowledge

_____
_____
_____
_____
_____
_____
_____
_____
_____

Results

_____
_____
_____
_____
_____
_____
_____
_____
_____

Week 33

Reaction Control

As customer service representatives, we come across a multitude of people with different feelings and behaviors. Customers are people too, so some may have had a bad day, or just are cranky in nature. Though we cannot control their behavior, we can control our reactions to them. A great customer service representative should always stay calm when handling customers, offering as much as they can to make them feel comfortable to express their concerns. A level head will not only quell the customer, but it may also reduce your own stress to help you move on to assist the next customer.

"Instead of asking others to change their behavior, your power is in your reaction to their behavior. You have no control over their behavior, but you do have complete control over your reaction to it."

Week 33

Applied Knowledge

_____
_____
_____
_____
_____
_____
_____
_____
_____
_____
_____

Results

_____
_____
_____
_____
_____
_____
_____
_____
_____
_____

Week 34

The Power of Thank You

In the vast world of commerce, chances are, your business is not the only business on the block. considering that consumers have a lot of options to choose from, it is always important we, as customer service professionals, make sure our clients feel appreciated. Even the smallest notion of gratitude can be the deciding factor on whether you earn someone's business or not. Writing a small thank you note, giving an extra effort to thank someone for calling, or even a small gift to celebrate accomplishments can greatly help sustain clientele and build a stronger rapport with customers.

"Thankfulness is the beginning of gratitude. Gratitude is the completion of thankfulness. Thankfulness may consist merely of words. Gratitude is shown in acts."

Week 34

Applied Knowledge

Results

Week 35

Having Thick Skin

In customer service, the ultimate goal is your customer's happiness. So, in times where the customer is irate, unreasonable or gives negative feedback, we need to understand that this is not personal. An expert customer service representative will have the ability to swallow his/her pride and handle these clients in a more empathetic way, with the understanding that there is truth to "the customer's always right". Just be human and level with your customers to give them assurance that you are doing the best that you can.

"Sometimes you have to shut up, swallow your pride and accept that you're wrong. It's not giving up, it's growing up."

Week 35

Applied Knowledge

Results

Week 36

Fail to Learn

No, I'm not asking you to quit learning. It's actually quite the contrary. This is one of the most basic principles in life, let alone when providing customer care, but it's also one of the most confusing concepts to grasp. Failing to learn is a system where failure must be experienced personally to benefit fully from learning. By using this method, essentially it will push you to want to do things on your own, correctly, the next time. Learning from your failures is an enriching process of self-awareness, and if you incorporate this principle in your daily customer service duties, it will help develop fine-tuned customer service that will always keep you ahead of the game.

"I never lose. Either I win or I learn"

Week 36

Applied Knowledge

_____
_____
_____
_____
_____
_____
_____
_____
_____
_____

Results

_____
_____
_____
_____
_____
_____
_____
_____
_____

Week 37

Volume Control

A useful tool that will help you control the tone of the call is controlling your volume. This works in 2 ways:

1. If you encounter an irate customer that raises his/her voice, you can speak in a lower volume and it generally helps control or lower the customer's volume as well.
2. Keeping a low volume when interacting with clients will help keep the conversation calm and cordial and prevents provoking a conflict.

Understand that it is not only WHAT you convey when providing customer service, but HOW it's conveyed that will determine the outcome.

"Speak your truth quietly and clearly; and listen to others, even to the dull and the ignorant, they too have their story."

Week 37

Applied Knowledge

_____
_____
_____
_____
_____
_____
_____
_____
_____
_____

Results

_____
_____
_____
_____
_____
_____
_____
_____
_____
_____

Week 38

If You Don't Know, Don't Let it Show

There are times where you will be asked something that you just do not know. We are not omniscient, so this is understandable. In these times, we want to at least demonstrate that we are willing to find the right answer, without admitting to a weakness. Use phrases such as, "Let me make sure I get the correct answer for you..." or, "That's a good question...", to show that you are interested in finding a solution to their concern/question, even when you didn't know the answer initially.

"The secret of man's success resides in his insight into the moods of people, and his tact in dealing with them."

Week 38

Applied Knowledge

_____
_____
_____
_____
_____
_____
_____
_____
_____
_____

Results

_____
_____
_____
_____
_____
_____
_____
_____
_____
_____

Week 39

Swear to Never Swear

All communication, whether verbal, written, or through body language, during customer service is crucial to the success of your interaction and business. Meanings of words or behaviors differ from place to place and culture to culture, where interpretation is left for the recipient to decide. To assure that your customer's experience is favorable, swearing (profanity), insults, and poor language should never be included in your customer service style. Using an inviting and informative approach, in a familiar manner will help retain a "down to earth" image, while keeping the interaction professional.

"A little consideration, a little thought for others, makes all the difference."

Week 39

Applied Knowledge

Results

Week 40

Practice Your Greeting

One of the most important parts of customer service is the "hello". Your greeting will determine the customer's comfortability with asking you for assistance. If you greet people in a friendly, inviting manner, there is a higher chance that the interaction will stay positive and the customer will naturally feel happy. Unfriendly greetings keep clients away and may determine whether they do business with you or not. Keep a smile, and always greet people politely.

"Sometimes you have to be kind to others, not because they're nice, but because you are."

Week 40

Applied Knowledge

Results

Week 41

Identify, Isolate, Overcome

This is one of the top core skills necessary for overcoming objections when dealing with anyone. Usually a sales tactic, it can easily be used in customer service to:

1. Identify the client's main concern by asking the correct questions.
2. Isolate the client's main concern by placing your focus solely on it.
3. Overcome the client's main concern by finding a solution and move forward.

It's important to know that finding a solution to overcome the concern could be just listening to a customer vent about a situation they've experienced or facilitating information that may not bring about an overall resolution. It all depends on what you identify as the main concern, and how you execute your next step.

"Challenges are what make life interesting and overcoming them is what makes life meaningful."

Week 41

Applied Knowledge

_____
_____
_____
_____
_____
_____
_____
_____
_____
_____

Results

_____
_____
_____
_____
_____
_____
_____
_____
_____
_____

Week 42

Don't Quit

It can be taxing when handling difficult situations in customer service, but not every day is the same. You are going to have days where you feel like you just can't lose, and other days where you just can't win. This does not mean you give up. Discipline and perseverance through times of struggle or maintaining a purpose despite obstacles will always lead towards growth and success. So, when times get rough...Pause, take a deep breath, and keep moving forward.

"A hero is an ordinary individual who finds the strength to persevere and endure in spite of overwhelming obstacles."

Week 42

Applied Knowledge

_____
_____
_____
_____
_____
_____
_____
_____
_____
_____

Results

_____
_____
_____
_____
_____
_____
_____
_____
_____
_____

Week 43

Think of Yourself Less, and Not Less of Yourself

In any human interaction, kindness is the universal language that demonstrates true consideration and respect for others. Therefore, a strong customer service representative always actively practices humility when handling clients. Respectfully considering others not only greatly impacts the mood and outcome of the interaction, but also encourages confidence in one's capabilities to be able to deal with situations in the best and most appropriate possible manner.

"Selfless action is a Source of strength."

Week 43

Applied Knowledge

_____
_____
_____
_____
_____
_____
_____
_____
_____
_____

Results

_____
_____
_____
_____
_____
_____
_____
_____
_____

Week 44

Make it a Habit, but the Right One

You may or may not know this about yourselves, but over 40 percent of your daily actions are not actual decisions, but a set or series of practiced habits. Habits are so powerful that the brain cannot tell the difference between bad and good habits and holds on to them at the exclusion of all other things, including common sense. This is why as Customer Service Representatives, it is our responsibility to choose the "right" things to form habits for as well as incorporate them into our service. Politeness, humility, and empathy are just some examples of the great virtues you should look to practice and make habits of to improve the service you provide clients.

"Success is neither magical nor mysterious. Success is the natural consequence of good habits."

Week 44

Applied Knowledge

Results

Week 45

Be Decisive, not Divisive

Every important skill to have in customer care is being able to produce positive results. So, with that in mind, interactions that result in discord should always be avoided. Skilled Customer service representatives utilize selective skills to create a good outcome in efforts to resolve the clients concerns or inquiries, and not to incite conflict. Always remain affably confident, while being focused and positive, during your decision-making process to help increase the potential of a favorable outcome.

"In a conflict, being willing to change allows you to move from a point of view to a viewing point. A higher, more expansive place, from which you can see both sides."

Week 45

Applied Knowledge

_____
_____
_____
_____
_____
_____
_____
_____
_____
_____
_____
_____

Results

_____
_____
_____
_____
_____
_____
_____
_____
_____
_____
_____
_____

Week 46

Know Your Objective

In order to be successful when interacting with people, one should always have the end result in mind. What is your desired outcome? What do you want to accomplish with the interaction? What obstacles might you encounter? What is your next step? These and other questions should be considered prior to interacting with clients to pave a path you can keep to in order to meet your ultimate goal.

"If you don't know where you are going, you might wind up someplace else."

Week 46

Applied Knowledge

_____
_____
_____
_____
_____
_____
_____
_____
_____
_____

Results

_____
_____
_____
_____
_____
_____
_____
_____
_____
_____

Week 47

Customers are People

In some cases, once you find that "groove" at your job, customer service may seem to become redundant. It is at these times we tend to fall into the trap of treating customers like numbers instead of individuals. Obviously, people do not want to be treated in this manner, in fact, 66% of customers would switch to another brand if they were to be treated like a number rather than an individual. Remember, without customers, businesses don't generate any profit, so make sure that each customer interaction is fresh and new with the understanding that customers are people.

"Never look down on anybody unless you're helping them up."

Week 47

Applied Knowledge

_____
_____
_____
_____
_____
_____
_____
_____
_____
_____

Results

_____
_____
_____
_____
_____
_____
_____
_____
_____
_____

Week 48

The Common Ground

When interacting with others, especially when providing customer service, it is very important to emphasize common ground. Identifying areas of agreement like stating, "I agree with you that..." or "We're on the same page that...", is a direct appeal to their sense of solidarity. Understand, however, assuming or presuming anything about the customer without establishing common ground, very well may emphasize distance. In these circumstances, ask indirect questions like, "So I believe you like cars, is that right?" or "Hey, you seem to appreciate good movies. Is this true?". Keeping a common ground will greatly improve the outcome of your customer interactions.

"Compassion gives us a common ground to stand on regardless of your faith background. It gives us a chance to stand shoulder-to-shoulder rather than go fist-to-fist with somebody."

Week 48

Applied Knowledge

_____
_____
_____
_____
_____
_____
_____
_____
_____
_____

Results

_____
_____
_____
_____
_____
_____
_____
_____
_____
_____

Week 49

Asking for Reasons

When dealing with others, sometimes the best way to show that you care about that person's thoughts and motivations is to ask them to explain their reasons, as long as you don't appear to be challenging them. If someone gives a statement of their opinion, ask them to elaborate on the subject, or ask leading questions to open the conversation. Every step closer to a humanistic connection with clients is worth taking in customer service.

"You can't judge my choices without understanding my reasons."

Week 49

Applied Knowledge

Results

Week 50

Ask P.O.Q.

Instead of thinking questions such as "Why can't I do this?", or, "Why is this not working?", try asking questions such as, "How can I figure the easiest way to do this?", or, "How can I make this work?". Your subconscious will always find an answer to questions you ask yourself, so asking yourself questions that are more positively oriented, your subconscious will find a more positive answer. Using the technique of consciously asking yourself positively oriented questions will teach you how to calmly work through your doubts and take actions on a positive basis.

"Positive questions bring out the best in people, inspire positive action, and create possibilities for positive futures."

Week 50

Applied Knowledge

Results

Week 51

Practice Your Craft

In most things, but particularly in every profession, for one to be able to thrive and excel, practice is not only a necessity, it is a requirement. From athletes to Actors and Lawyers to Accountants, refreshing the mind through practice keeps them in tune with their expertise and constantly "in the know". The next time you have the opportunity, practice your communications skills and try to identify how others react or what shows to be more effective in situations like:

- Speaking to a stranger- For instance at the grocery story, or while waiting on line.
- Interacting with co-workers- While at a company party or in the break room at lunch.
- Talking to family and close friends- At a holiday family function, a cookout or at home with your wife and children.

Remember, you can become really good with practice, especially when you are practicing good.

"Practice makes perfect. After a long time of practicing, our work will become natural, skillful, swift, and steady."

Applied Knowledge

Week 51

_____

_____
_____
_____
_____
_____
_____
_____
_____
_____

Results

_____
_____
_____
_____
_____
_____
_____
_____
_____

Week 52

Paraphrase to Their Approval

One of the best ways to let customers know that you are actively listening to them is to paraphrase back to them your interpretation of what they are saying. The paraphrasing is to emphasize the essence of their concern, question, or situation to get affirmation that you are on the same page. This gives the client better assurance and confidence in you being able to address their specific situation and may keep the interaction cordial.

"Effective communication starts with being able to listen, not speak."

Week 52

Applied Knowledge

_____
_____
_____
_____
_____
_____
_____
_____
_____
_____

Results

_____
_____
_____
_____
_____
_____
_____
_____
_____
_____

www.ingramcontent.com/pod-product-compliance
Lightning Source LLC
Chambersburg PA
CBHW032057150426

43194CB00006B/562